CHORDS OF COMFORT

Chords of Comfort

Unlocking Life's Lessons of Healing through Music

A person does not experience God's presence through sadness or laziness, but through joy as it is written regarding the Prophet Elisha who said: "Now bring a musician to me – and when the musician played, the hand of God was upon him." (II Kings 3:15)

Rabbi Ron Isaacs

KTAV PUBLISHING HOUSE

Contents

I dedicate this book to all those beautiful people and their families who allowed me to play music for them.

Foreword

What does a Rabbi do for retirement? While I am nowhere near knowing the answer to that question, I imagine many would take the time to find personal modes of spiritual growth. After a life of giving to others, we would presume the rabbi be content with the new period of quiet. However, when it comes to my colleague Rabbi Ron Isaacs, our image would be wrong. Rabbi Isaacs has taken an entirely different retirement path. As he was preparing for his retirement from over 40 years as the Rabbi of Temple Sholom in Bridgewater, NJ, we met for lunch at the now closed Kosher Chinese restaurant in Manville, NJ to discuss his desire to continue giving to others through the power of music. On that day we began the journey of creating "Chords of Comfort," Rabbi Isaacs' retirement gig as a guitar player for the terminally ill.

As we know, the ideal care model in medicine is caring for all aspects of an individual, the mind, body and spirit. This holistic focus on people includes finding ways to connect that go beyond the simple dialogue towards which we naturally gravitate. With the inclusion of Rabbi Isaacs and his "Chords of Comfort," we at Stein Hospice and the Oscar and Ella Wilf

Campus for Senior Living were fortunate to expand how we could connect to people in their final weeks and months of life. Through the five years he has provided his music to our patients and families, Rabbi Isaacs has truly found ways to connect to people, to bring moments of joy into the midst of despairing periods of life and truly engage people's spirit and mind through music. I am proud to have him as colleague and grateful for his care of our patients and families through these years. May Rabbi Isaacs continue to have many years of health and love for playing his guitar as he continues to raise up people's spirits.

Rabbi Bryan Kinzbrunner, BCC
Director of Religious and Spiritual Services, Oscar and Ella Wilf Campus for Senior Living
President, Neshama; Association of Jewish Chaplains
President, Rabbinic Association in the Heart of New Jersey

*Music gives a soul to the universe, wings to
the mind and life to everything (Plato)*

Introduction

Nothing affects the human being more than music. By
happenstance, a person can hear a certain melody at a
time of personal sadness or joy and then let the melody pass
out of his mind. Years later, that person may hear that same
melody only to be overpowered by the emotional sadness or
joy he experienced when he first heard the melody.

Music is powerful. Music does not forget. Memory never
entirely recedes, and music may summon it. Some music
inspires you to move your arms, feet and legs. There is no
doubt that music moves people in special ways. Medical stud-
ies over the years have confirmed that music can sometimes
actually lift people out of their Alzheimer's haze and bring
them back to some semblance of normality, albeit for a short
period of time.

A moment that profoundly changed my life occurred early
on in my rabbinic career when a close cousin with whom I

had spent many weekends as a college undergraduate had a massive stroke. I visited him at a hospital in New York City after he fell ill. There he was, lying in bed with his wife at his bedside. When I spoke to him, I sadly realized that he was no longer able to speak even though it appeared that he was understanding what I was saying.

Weeks later after some rehabilitation my cousin returned home. I continued to call him on the phone each week. The conversations were one way; I did all the talking. Then came that unforgettable *aha* moment when I called him and spontaneously sang the question to him "how are you feeling?" To my great surprise and shock, he sang back to me "I am feeling fine!" I now realized that we could talk to each other using melody. There was a musical part of his brain that allowed him to speak in song. All my subsequent visits and conversations were conducted in song. We both felt spiritually uplifted, and my cousin did too. Song had unlocked the secret to his communication.

After my retirement from the congregational rabbinate I became a bedside musician for a local Jewish hospice. Known as "Chords of Comfort", I visit people wherever they reside, singing and playing guitar. I often bring rhythm instruments with me and invite patients who are able to use them to help keep the beat. My experiences have been deep, mystical and spiritual. and I have learned many life lessons from my amazing patients. I have personally experienced how music can offer a spiritual healing to those struggling with illness. These experiences have profoundly affected and inspired me, and I hope my records of these encounters will touch you.

RHI

Year One

My Journey Begins

"Do not look at the flask but at its contents" (Ethics of the Fathers 4:27)

CHAPTER 1

The Famous Journalist: Day One

I remember waking up on the first morning of paying a visit to my first patient. I was excited about the unknown adventure that would await me. What would be the response to my music? Would it be a positive experience for my patient? Would my repertoire of songs be the right mix? I had a light breakfast (always best not to overeat before singing) and headed out with guitar in hand. Arriving at the nursing home I was given the room number of Mr. G. but when I arrived at the room there was no one in bed. I returned to the nursing station and was told that he was sitting in a corner of the hallway in his wheelchair.

Seated in his wheelchair in a hallway, I approached him, introduced myself and told him that I came to play music especially for him. I remember him shouting: "What are you doing here? What do you want? Go away." (Not what I expected on my first day on the job).

I had traveled quite a distance to see him, so I decided that I simply needed to take a deep breath and show patience. After a few minutes of sitting next to him I asked him whether I could return him to his room and at least talk and let him know who I was and why I came to visit. For a few moments there was complete silence. And then much to my surprise he agreed! One of the aides helped wheel him into his room.

As I have always learned to do, I peruse the room where the patient resides which is often filled with pictures and memorabilia. Many of these helps tell the story of his life. I looked around and saw a picture of Mr. G. as a young man in the army, and a picture of his family and wife. (I later learned that his wife was also a resident in the same facility but had dementia and living in a separate room). These pictures gave me an opportunity to ask him things about his life. He did respond in short sentences to each of my queries. Now it was time to offer him some of my music.

After singing my first song ("You are my sunshine") I asked Mr. G. to tell me some things about his life. He said that he was a journalist for the New York Times and wrote lots of books. When I asked him to name some of his books, he was unable to do so. He also told me that he was a speech writer for many famous people, knew former President Richard Nixon and wrote speeches for Vice President Spiro Agnew. I was skeptical, although his detailed description of the West Wing struck me as plausible.

When I told him that I was from Canada and spoke French he started to speak some French to me. I asked him "Parlez vous francaise?" (Do you speak French) and he answered "Un peu" (just a little). It was then that I sang him the French song Frere Jacques and he joined in singing it with me. My first success! And thus, our friendship began with weekly visits, Frere Jacques as my warmup song and speaking French. Each time we sang some songs and he talked about the many books that he wrote, and his many trips oversees to France where he learned to speak French. Still I was skeptical.

In the fourth month of my visits his health was transitioning, and he died peacefully soon thereafter. Such is the life of a bedside musician who performs for people in hospice. As it says in the Book of Job, God gives, and God takes away. It was after his death that I decided to do some research to see if any of the things that he told me were true. With the help of the internet I would later learn that he indeed taught at the prestigious Columbia University School of Journalism, wrote many books and articles and in fact was a speech writer for Vice President Spiro Agnew!

I always knew in my heart that one should never judge a book by its cover. I shall always remember Mr. G and was thankful to have been privileged to meet him and offer him companionship and my music. By establishing a relationship of trust with him he allowed me to visit him each week and spend time in conversation and song.

The joy of the heart begets song
(Zohar Book of Mysticism ii, 93a)

CHAPTER 2

America the Beautiful

I was now into my second month of making patient rounds as a bedside musician. Most of my patients that I was asked to play for resided in nursing homes and assisted living facilities. Today I was on my way to make my first house visit to a lady (Mrs. B) who lived about 25 miles from where I reside. Things had been going well and I felt that I was making a positive impact through my songs and guitar playing. There was generally some reaction to my music (hand movements and foot stomping to rhythmic songs) and sometimes conversation and singing along depending upon the health of my patient.

Arriving in the late morning I knocked on the door and a man whose name was Fred answered. He was in particularly good shape for his age (a man in his eighties), and as I passed the hallway, I saw many medallions that he had amassed in swimming competitions. He had me seated in his living room while his wife was being served a late breakfast by the hospice aide. Fred told me about his life, his wonderful marriage to his wife and how her memory slowly began to fail her seven years ago. For the past couple of years, she was totally uncommunicative, and the only time Fred ever got to leave the home was for a one hour swim each day at a local YMCA.

When I told Fred that I was a rabbi who had served a congregation for 40 years he was extremely excited. He told me about his synagogue which was small and struggling to attract new members, and how excited he was that a new young rabbi was trying to grow his congregation by instituting new programs, such as musical services held outdoors and visits to a local shopping mall where the rabbi sat at a table that had an Ask the Rabbi sign. It was a kind of open house where people had an opportunity to ask the rabbi a question over a cup of coffee. It was quite apparent that my time with Fred not only afforded him companionship but a small break from having to be around the clock caregiver to his wife.

After some time, the aide came into the living room and told us that Mrs. B. had finished her lunch. Fred and I went into the kitchen, sat down next to Mrs. B. and I began to play and sing some of my songs. I even brought a small tambourine and asked Fred to accompany me which he genuinely enjoyed. After playing the first song I turned to Mrs. B. and said: "How did you like the music?" Mrs. B. looked at me with eyes wide open but no response. Throughout the playing of my repertoire of songs there was minimal response – little hand or foot movement and not a single word spoken.

My final song that morning was an original song for peace that I had written. I wished Mrs. B. a good week and left the house. Fred thanked me and told me how much he appreciated my visit and looked forward to my next visit, which was going to be again on a Friday.

On my way driving home I thought about this loving couple, and how Fred's life for the past seven years had changed from one of loving husband to that of loving caregiver with a wife who had lost her memory. I thought that even though I was unsure as to whether my music was resonating with Mrs. B. that my time with Fred was important to him. He now had something to look forward to each week as I became a trusted friend who offered a listening ear as well as companionship.

The first imperative of Judaism is "Live life." But when living becomes difficult, the next thing one can do for another is to care. Caring is where healing resides. Visiting the ill is a religious obligation, considered one of Judaism's ultimate acts of kindness. Its underlying ethos is the dignity of the human being, the respect for one's suffering, and the power to restore dignity to the patient.

Each week, on a late Friday morning I would continue to drive to Fred's home to play music for Mrs. B. My visit would start in the living room in conversation with Fred, who by this time was asked by his rabbi to talk about his experience of living with a wife who has dementia and sharing his observations with my visits at his synagogue. This gave Fred a purpose and an opportunity to join with his fellow congregants in offering some advice related to care giving.

Later in the morning Mrs. B would finish her breakfast and we would both go into the kitchen where I would sing for her while strumming my guitar.

Toward the end of June, I would make one final visit to Fred and Mrs. B. before I went away on vacation. Little could I know that this visit was going to be one for the ages and change every visit that was to follow. The routine was the same – first in the living room with Fred and then in the kitchen to sing my songs. Since July 4th was soon approaching, I thought it would be nice to sing Mrs. B. a patriotic song. I chose America the Beautiful. I had come to learn when preparing to take the test for my American citizenship (I was born in Toronto, Canada) that America the Beautiful was written in the late 1800s by an English professor as a poem to commemorate the Fourth of July. By 1900 at least 7500 different melodies had been written to the poem, but the one by Samuel A. Ward, a church organist and choir director is still the most popular one today. It is a most beautiful song and poem.

And so, I began to sing: "O beautiful, for spacious skies for amber waves of grain."

Suddenly out of the mouth of Mrs. B. comes: "For purple mountain majesties, above the fruited plain."

Fred and I are both shocked as Mrs. B. continues to sing along with me the rest of the song: "America, America. God shed his grace on thee. And crown thy good with brotherhood from sea to shining sea." Tears of joy now drip down Fred's face. When I asked Mrs. B: "Did you like the song, she answered and said: "Very good!" Mrs. B. is not only singing but talking! It was a spiritual moment for all of us, and a feeling of appreciating one of the daily miracles of life, being able to communicate. I went home that day to prepare for the Sabbath thinking about how that one song triggered an awakening for Mrs. B that had been dormant all those years.

When I returned from vacation, I continued to visit Fred and Mrs. B. She sang along to many of my songs, moved her arms in rhythm to the beat of a song and spoke in short sentences. Music had given Mrs. B a new soul and a new spirit. It was during one of my visits that I told Fred that I was planning to take a congregational trip to Israel. For the past twenty plus years my wife and I organized and designed a trip to Israel for members of my congregation. It was a wonderful opportunity to get to know congregants more personally and share with them the beautiful State of Israel. Fred had always wanted to visit Israel with his wife but was never able to do so. When I asked Fred whether he would like to join my trip he unhesitatingly said that if he could get family coverage for his wife that he would love to do so. That March Fred did travel to Israel with me (he also took along one of his grandsons) and had the time of his life. He prayed for his wife at the Western Wall and enjoyed his first vacation in many years.

A few months later Mrs. B. died while I was away on vacation out of state. Fred called me to ask whether I would be able to come to her funeral. Unfortunately, I was not able to attend but wrote a eulogy to her memory that was read by the hospice chaplain who is a rabbinic colleague of mine. In time of illness we will all need supportive and caring friends who will talk and listen and even allow us to climb upon their shoulders for spiritual sustenance. I was so honored to have made the acquaintances of Fred and his beloved wife Mrs. B. It was an honor and a privilege to be invited into her home each week to sing and play for her. To her memory I will continue to sing all the days of my life.

Remembrance brings actions in its train (Talmud, Menachot 13)

CHAPTER 3
Take Me Out to the Ball Game

A s I prepared to see my next patient, I could never have imagined that baseball would be his topic for the next four months. Baseball is by far my favorite sport. Growing up as a child I had a professional baseball player living across the road from me. On days when he was home, he would hit high pop ups to a group of my friends on our street with a sponge ball. I was now totally hooked on the game and thus began an obsession for collecting baseball cards.

Growing up in Toronto Canada we only had minor league baseball. Nevertheless, my father took me to a few games, and I loved the action and the popcorn. On most weekends during baseball season my closest childhood friend and I would gather next to our small black and white tv set and watch the

Yankee broadcast. As they began to amass World Series after World Series rings, I was convinced that the Yankees would be my favorite team. From now on I would "root root root" for the Yankees" who would become my home team.

In the mid 1960s when I began my college career in New York I finally got to see my first major league game at Yankee stadium. It was magical and the immensity of the stadium as compared to Toronto was mind boggling. At the same time, I began to continue my hobby of collecting baseball cards and attending baseball card conventions. I got to meet Mickey Mantle at one of the shows and got him to sign a baseball. It is now one of my priceless possessions.

Thirty years ago, in 1989 I went to see the movie Field of Dreams at a drive-in theatre. It was a crisp cool summer evening and all the cars were lined up in their parking spaces with the speakers situated near each car's front window. It was another magical evening and I loved the movie with all its intriguing fantasy. "If you build it, he will come," is what Ray Kinsella, a novice farmer hears several times over the course of days from a bodiless voice emanating from somewhere in his cornfield in Iowa. No one else hears the voice, and later he has a vision that the mysterious voice is none other than Shoeless Joe Jackson, infamous for throwing games during the 1919 World Series in exchange for money. Ray grew up with baseball and his long-deceased father played in the minor leagues in 1919. Ray was estranged from his father and decides to tear up part of his corn field to build that baseball field. And the players of old come back to play at the corn field, including Ray's own father.

I was unprepared to enter into another fantasy game of baseball when I came to play music for my patient, an Italian fellow named Mr. K. He was fully able to communicate with me in complete sentences and enjoyed my first visit very much, with lots of smiles on his face and a special grin when I was able to sing him a short song in Italian. But it was when I sang for him "Take Me Out to the Ballgame", one of my signature songs that things began to change. Not only did he sing along with me, with his hands waving back and forth, but he began to introduce me to people on his imaginary baseball field. He said to me, I'd like you to meet my brother Fred, one of my teammates who plays shortstop. "Nice to meet you," I responded.

I began to "play along" with Mr. K's interest in his baseball game. I talked to him about the position he played, his batting average, how often he played his games. Mr. K. insisted he was the fastest man on his team, and when he got a hit, it was an automatic double since he was able to steal second base with lightning speed.

The next time I came to visit Mr. K. his daughter and granddaughter were visiting as well. After introducing myself to the family I encouraged them to join me in song. Once we sang "Take Me Out to the Ballgame" Mr. K. began talking about his memories of the next game. He introduced us all to some of the players on his team, the favorite foods that were being sold at the stadium and told us how he was the most valuable player. I asked him the details of his batting stance, with which pitches he had the most success, and how often he practiced. He remembered so many things, including the grip that he had on the ball when he made his throws from shortstop to first base. It was obvious how much he enjoyed the game and his get-togethers with his fellow teammates.

Several months went by and I continued to make my weekly visits. Over time his health began to deteriorate, and he was unable to stay communicative for long periods of time. During my last couple of visits, he was sleeping upright in his wheelchair. I did all the talking and singing, and would always end with "and it's one, two three strikes you're out at the old ball game."

Memory is a gift afforded to human beings. It is human nature to enjoy reminiscing about memorable events in our lives. That is why we celebrate birthdays and anniversaries, and in the Jewish faith light a candle on the anniversary of the death of our loved ones. It was a wonderful opportunity for me to be able to join in the baseball memories of Mr. K. They were times when he was happy with the camaraderie of teammates and a game he excelled in playing. He loved his time on the baseball field.

On the entrance to the Yad Va-shem Holocaust Memorial in Jerusalem there are these words by the great Rabbi Nachman of Breslov: "In remembering is the secret of redemption." We become a community and are held together as a people by common remembering. I shall always remember Mr. K. as the man who loved the game of baseball and the man who was the "fastest guy in baseball."

A person should feed his animals before
eating (Talmud Berachot 40a)

CHAPTER 4
My Favorite Pets

*R*esearch of the National Pet Owners survey has shown that sixty-two percent of all Americans own a pet: 78 million dogs and 86 million cats. This is an amazing statistic. Today one can purchase pet insurance, pet beds, pet clothing, pet houses and pet toys. There are pet cemeteries, pet spas, pet vacations, pet meds and a wide variety of premium pet foods, even kosher ones. I am the proud owner of a beautiful golden retriever. Most pet owners, including this author, consider their pet to be a member of their family. Many of those in my neighborhood who have a pet have told me that their dogs tried to make them feel better when they were unhappy. I too am a believer. My life has been far more satisfying and less stressful due in part to having Reba my golden retriever in my home.

As a rabbi of a synagogue for four decades, I have had

the pleasure of meeting many of my congregants' pets when visiting their homes. I have witnessed the joy that they have brought to their family, the Hebrew names that some have been given, and I have comforted bereaved families that have lost their pets. In the next couple of months in my work as Chords of Comfort I was soon to learn firsthand how animals have served my patients therapeutically.

The day of this memorable visit was filled with a bright and sunny sky as I set out to visit a new patient in his home. Mr. B's wife greeted me at the door, as did a beautiful German shepherd. Mrs. B. led me to her husband's room and the dog followed. To my great surprise, when I began to strum my first song on the guitar the dog started to sing in a high howling pitch. Throughout the song she was singing as Mr. B. lay in his bed with a big smile on his face.

Mr. B. was somewhat communicative and sang along to many of the songs which I knew would be well known to him. But it was Rex, the German Shepherd by his side that really helped with his pastoral care. As Mr. B. lay in bed stroking the fur of his pet it was obvious to me how much he adored him and his companionship. There was a loving bond in evidence that added to the impact of my playing guitar and singing him songs. Even Rex seemed to enjoy the music!

Later that same day I was to visit several of my patients at a local assisted living. When I arrived a therapy Labrador retriever was making his rounds to a gathering of people in the television social hall. The well-trained pooch was taken around to all of the residents in attendance. They all seemed to really enjoy this loving companion. At that point I decided to take my guitar from its case and play "How much is that doggie in the window." Many joined in the singing and the therapy dog appeared to enjoy the music as well.

My next visit was to a patient in her room who was sitting on her rocking chair with a cat in her lap. It was not a real cat, but one of those therapy pet toys. I introduced myself and Mrs. K. began telling me about herself and family. I asked about her cat, and she told me it was soon to be lunch time and time for it to be fed. As she was petting its fur the cat made a "meow" sound and rolled over in her arms. It even began to purr and admittedly I had never seen such a realistic looking cat. (I was so impressed with it that later that week I bought a therapy cat of my own which I travel with on many of my visits to patients.) I pulled out my guitar and sang one of my signature songs that often bring back fond childhood memories – "Old MacDonald Had a Farm." And so I sang: "And on his farm he had a cat, E-I-E-I-O. And a meow meow here, a meow meow there...." Much to my amazement the therapy cat not only purred but was able to make the meow sound as it was being stroked on its back. Mrs. K. loved the song and sang along as I added more verses of animal after animal sound.

As the weeks went by, I decided to continue bringing my therapy cat to patients along with my guitar. Several of my patients on my home visits had their own therapy pet toy which they admired and loved as if it were real. But one of my most memorable home visits regarding an animal was a visit to Mrs. S. who had her cat laying with her in bed when I arrived. Mrs. S. was not very communicative and was nearing the end of her days. Her daughter was also present, and I begin to play some very tranquil songs. With eyes wide opened Mrs. S. listened to my singing and playing but was unable to verbally communicate, except for her feet which were moving to the rhythm of my song. As I was about to leave, I decided to end my time with Mrs. S. and sang her "Twinkle twinkle little star." As I was finishing the song, I noticed that both Mrs.

S. and her cat had fallen asleep and both were in dreamland. It was a great ending to a wonderful day of singing music and witnessing the power of therapy pets.

Anyone who has ever owned a pet knows what a good friend a pet can be and how a pet can help diffuse stress in one's life. Having a family pet has the additional educational benefit of teaching children how to care for another creature. George Eliot once wrote that "animals are such agreeable friends – they ask no questions; they pass no criticism." I could not agree more.

Over these past five years I have seen the power of having a living pet or a therapy animal toy. Some of my patients could have visitations of their pets to the nursing home. I have watched as their souls were uplifted as their dog or cat was brought to their room. They literally lit up the room. As a rabbi I have been asked whether animals have souls. All my dogs that I have ever had in my life surely have had a soul. They have been uplifting to have as loving companions and have been the light of my life. As Proverbs 20:27 reminds us: The soul is God's candle. My dogs have been my light, and my patients' dogs and cats have been their light too! And the combination of music and pet therapy is a winning one for sure.

*There is a Temple in Heaven that is only opened
through song (Tikkune Zohar 45a)*

CHAPTER 5

The Singers

*E*ver since primitive people learned to create musical
sounds and instruments, instrumental music and song
have carried special significance. This has been especially
true for the Jewish people. The biblical record is full of the
idea that it is natural for people to burst forth spontaneously
into song when moved by signs and wonders of God. Moses,
Miriam, Deborah and King David, the "sweet singer of the
Israelites" – all celebrated personal deliverance in song and
dance. Rabbinic thinkers considered music and song to be
ways by which the people served God in joy and gladness.
Vocal music to this day has remained an essential component
of Jewish prayer.

I received my first gift of guitar the year I became a Bar
Mitzvah. Because I was fortunate to inherit my mother's

beautiful voice, I taught myself how to play and began entertaining people at synagogue events and nursing homes as a volunteer. Singing has always been an important part of my life and there have been several memorable times that I have had with patients who were incredible singers. In my first year as Chords of Comfort I had the pleasure of visiting Mr. F. at a local nursing home. Arriving at his room he was already listening to music on his CD player. I introduced myself and asked whether I could sit down and have a chat, and even play some songs for him. He was most agreeable, and I pulled out my guitar from its case and began to play. He immediately sang along, and it was evident to me that he had a beautiful voice. I thought that he must have had voice lessons and asked whether that was so. He replied that he just loved to sing and that his siblings all had great voices. It was then that he turned to me and asked: "Would you like me to sing you a song?" This was unexpected, and I answered "of course!"

It was then that he put a new CD into his player which was filled with instrumental music only. I realized that this was to be a karaoke performance and he began to sing his first song while I, who had been expecting to sing to him, simply listened in total amazement. His singing seemed to take him back to his childhood and as I watched his facial expressions it became obvious to me that he had forgotten about his illness and was living in the moment with the music that he so much loved to sing. After his first song I applauded him in approval. He then moved on to a second and third song. How ironic – I who had come to play and sing for him was now being serenaded by my patient.

It turned out to be a memorable day, with lots of positive conversation and singing along. Yes, I did manage to get a couple of songs of mine into the mix which he enjoyed. I was now about to visit my next newest patient and could hardly wait for what would become my next adventure.

That afternoon I went to another nursing home where my almost 100-year-old patient, Mrs. F. awaited me. An extremely sweet woman, she was able to fully converse with me and after I introduced myself as the singing rabbi, I asked whether I could play some songs for her. My first song which I often use to begin sessions was "You are my sunshine". She knew it well and smiled along and clapped her hands as I sang the first verse of the song. Then came my next big surprise. I started with the next verse of the song: "I'll always love you and make you happy, if you will only say the same ... " Mrs. F. began to sing with me, but not only did she sing with full knowledge of all the words, she sang the song in harmony with me, as if we were performing as a duo. Her daughter was in the room with us and was also delighted with the engagement and participation of her mother. When we both finished singing, I asked her how she knew how to sing the harmony line of the song. She said that she had always sung in the choir and talked to me about its four-part harmony whenever they performed a song.

We continued to sing songs harmoniously and there were more smiles on Mrs. F. and her daughter's face that one could possibly imagine. I too was having the time of my life, knowing how the music transformed her and enabled her to almost imagine that she was back in time singing with her choir. As the day went on, I kept thinking about the ability of Mrs. F to sing each and every song with me in perfect harmony. Which led me to end my session with her with this well-known song from the 1970s which was part of the Coca-Cola campaign. It was called "I'd like to Teach the World to Sing" but had an alternate title "In Perfect Harmony:"

"I'd like to build the world a home
And furnish it with love
Grow apple trees and honeybees
And snow-white turtle doves

I'd like to teach the world to sing
In perfect harmony
I'd like to hold it in my arms
And keep it company. "

It's the real thing, what the world wants today,
That's the way it will stay, it's the real thing.

My special day with Mrs. F. was the real thing. It again affirmed how music can stimulate the brain and provide a brain workout. Research has shown that listening to music can reduce anxiety, blood pressure and pain, as well as improve mental alertness and memory. I witnessed firsthand the power of music on this day of two special singers. American musician Billy Joel, one of my favorite vocalists and musicians once said: "I think music in itself has healing power. It is an explosive expression of humanity. It is something we are all touched by. No matter what culture we are from, everyone loves music." I whole heartedly agree with this statement of the performer known as the "piano man," and it is this universal bond with music that has led researchers across the globe to continue to investigate its therapeutic potential. I do not need any additional proof.

Year Two
(Adding Rhythm Instruments)

Praise God with the blasts of the horn. Praise God with harp and lyre (Psalm 150:3)

CHAPTER 1

Family Band

I can hardly believe that one year has now passed since I began my new work as a bedside musician, offering my music and song to people in hospice. I found my first year very fulfilling and was excited about the new adventures that I knew were awaiting me. I felt that my many experiences in year one would benefit me in knowing how to deal with patients of many different health challenges and capabilities. And it was always exhilarating when I first entered the room of a new patient, not ever knowing what to expect, and often experiencing the unexpected. This visit was going to be one of those *aha* moments.

In addition to often carrying with me to visits my therapeutic cat, I decided that I would bring with me a couple of rhythm instruments – a drum, sets of maracas, and tambourines so that my patients might have an opportunity to

participate in the music by playing rhythm. My first patient
was a woman who had lost her vision and ability to communicate. I set out on my drive and arrived at the assisted living
facility where my patient resided. I took the elevator up to
the second floor and proceeded down a long hallway. As I
got closer to the room in which my patient resided there was
what sounded like live music emitting from her room. Upon
arriving at the room of Mrs. P. I poked my head inside and
at and around her bedside was a small quartet of people – a
flutist, a guitar player, a drummer and a young vocalist. I had
thought perhaps that the medical team for Mrs. P. might have
ordered alternative music therapy of which I was unaware.
(My hospice also provides an outstanding harpist as part of
its musical therapy). I introduced myself to the musicians and
told them I would come back another time. After all, they were
already doing an amazing job. To my surprise they invited
me into the room and asked me to join in the ensemble. I
asked who they were, and to my surprise they were all family
members related to Mrs. P: a daughter (playing the flute) a
son-in-law, (guitar) and a granddaughter who had flown in
from San Francisco and with her mellifluous voice offered
her song. They introduced me to Mrs. P. who was lying in bed,
eyes closed but obviously paying attention to the music since
she was swaying back and forth in bed. I placed one of my
tambourines in her hand and asked the group what their next
song would be. It was one of my favorites – a Carol King classic,
and it was not long before all of us – now a mini orchestra
were playing together for Mrs. P. My fellow musicians were
nothing short of amazing, and the lead singer had a trained
soprano voice. It was a beautiful sight to behold – a family
that had come to visit their loved one fulfilling the mitzvah
of *bikkur holim* – visiting the sick and offering a pleasurable
sensory experience for Mrs. P. Throughout our time together

I watched as Mrs. P. moved her arms and legs to the rhythm of the songs, while tapping on the tambourine that I had placed in her hand. Her lying in bed with family gathered around her reminded me of the biblical Jacob at the end of the Book of Genesis who is lying in bed with only days to live with all his children gathered around him.

The Jewish people have been called "the people of the book," but they are just as surely the people of the family. As a people they began with Abraham, Isaac Jacob and the matriarchs Sarah, Rebekah, Rachel, Leah and their children. Mrs. P's children understood the importance of family, and it was especially heartwarming to learn that her young grand-daughter had made the trip all the way from San Francisco to offer her voice, sweet as a nightingale, in order to give her grandmother the pleasures of music.

Throughout most of Jewish history, the important religious commandment of visiting the sick was binding upon all its people. Jewish communities even established "Visiting of the Sick Societies" to ensure visitations to all sick people. Recognizing how psychologically important it is that the sick should not feel abandoned, the rabbis declared that whoever visits a sick person removes one sixtieth of his illness (Talmud, Baba Metzia 30b.) In fact, among all of the many religious obligations in Judaism, visiting of the sick would likely be among God's top ten. It is one of the deeds of kindness which was said to yield immediate fruit and continue to yield fruit in time to come.

It was not too many weeks after paying my first visit to Mrs. P. that she died. The family sent me a beautiful thank you note in which they told me how much they appreciated my many visits. I shall forever remember the joy of offering my music to Mrs. P. and having the honor to be asked to become a member of her family band.

Back in times of the Jerusalem Temple it was the Levites who were chosen to serve as the singers. The Book of Jewish Mysticism states that the name "Levi" means cleaving, and that the soul of those who heard the singing at once cleaved to God. Being among the singers that sang for Mrs. P enabled our spirits to be raised. It was a magical spiritual experience and made all of us feel a little bit closer to the One on High.

Let the honor of your friend be as dear to you
as your own. (Ethics of the Fathers 2:15)

CHAPTER 2

Playing for a Friend

*P*eople often say that they have many acquaintances, but
there are few people who admit to having more than
one or two close friends. The Hebrew word *chaver* is used in
rabbinic writings to mean a friend, but this word has many
other connotations as well, including colleague, associate,
partner, companion and fellow.

Friendship is an important value in Judaism. The friendship of David and Jonathan as portrayed in the first book of
Samuel is held in high esteem. In this friendship, both David
and Jonathan give totally of themselves to each other but do
not make demands upon the other. Because such friendships
are unusual, we are urged to be careful in choosing our own
friends.

Each morning I go to my computer to check on the list
of those patients for whom music is recommended. Almost

each and every day the list changes as people pass away and
new ones are added to my play list. As it says in the Book of
Job, "God gives, and God takes away." Up until now all the
people that I have been playing music for were not known to
me before I ever met them. But on this particular day as I was
perusing my list, I came across a name of one of my acquaintances, which admittedly came as a shock to me. I did not
know that he had been diagnosed with cancer. Furthermore, I
had so admired him as a fellow musician and guitar player who
composed many original melodies and appeared in a band
that performed in area synagogues and Jewish Community
Centers. He had given me one of his recordings which I was
constantly listening to in the car. And I had used some of his
original melodies which he wrote to prayers in my worship
services.

My friend had home hospice care as the family decided
that this would be the best place for him to spend his remain-
ing days. And so, I called his wife who I did not know well,
introduced myself and told her that I would like to come
and visit her husband and play some songs for him. She told
me what day would be best that week, and so it was on a
Wednesday morning that I headed over to his home. All the
while I was thinking – what kind of songs would I play for
him? Should I play songs that he wrote, and if so, would I do
justice to playing and singing them? I began to sing one of my
melodies that he wrote while in the car. Singing helped my
own personal tension of not knowing what to expect when I
arrived at his home.

I rang the doorbell and his wife answered. Inviting me in,
she showed me to his bed which was situated in the living
room. My friend ("J") was much less robust than the last
time I saw him. When he looked up from his bed, he gave
me a smile, and I asked whether I could play some songs

for him. He was pleased to have me do so. I had a playlist of possible songs in my mind and decided that I would sing a lot of Hebrew songs since those were the ones that he most enjoyed performing while in his singing group. My first song was a version of Adon Olam – Lord of the World, the prayer which ends most Jewish worship services. I especially like the last verse which basically translates that "when I go to sleep at night, I have nothing to fear. Body and soul are in God's hands." He seemed to approve and whispered some words to me indicating his pleasure in having me come to visit. Needless to say, it warmed my heart to hear this.

One of his original melodies is one that I so much enjoyed using at my worship services. It is a song and prayer for peace in Israel and for all who dwell on earth, and his version was a very tranquil one. The Hebrew word "shalom" has many meanings, including hello, goodbye and peace. But I have also understood the word to mean "to your health", and so I took a deep breath and played for him his original tune. As I played, I closed my eyes and prayed that my voice and singing would help to soothe his soul and offer him a modicum of healing. The song went well, or so I thought. As soon as I finished playing his wife called out to me: "I think that one of your strings was out of tune when you sang that song." My guitar had been tuned before arriving at their home and I thought that my guitar was well tuned. In any event, I took the constructive criticism to mean that I should take a break and retune my guitar strings. And that is exactly what I did.

After about a half hour of playing songs with some conversation it was obvious to me that it would soon be time for me to leave, since he was slowly fading and ready to close his eyes and go to sleep. With his facial motions as my guidelines I chose an original song that I had written for my last song. Its words are: "Let there be peace, let there be peace, let there be peace in the whole wide world. Shalom, Shalom bechol ha'olam." Upon finishing the song, he was in dreamland. I spent a few minutes talking to his wife in the kitchen before taking leave and she thanked me one hundred-fold for taking the time to make a home visit and offer my song and guitar.

Centuries ago, Rabbi Eliezer ben Yitzchak wrote several guidelines to advise those who were visiting the sick: "Visit the sick and lighten their suffering. Pray for them and leave. Do not stay too long, for you may inflict upon them additional discomfort. And when you visit those who are ill, always enter the room cheerfully." I felt that my actions this day would have been approved by this great rabbi.

Awake and arise to greet the new light. (Lecha Dodi)

CHAPTER 3

"Are You Sleeping?"

*M*any years ago, I read a fascinating book called "Awakenings", written by Dr. Oliver Sachs, a professor of clinical neurology at Albert Einstein Medical School. Sachs chronicles his experience with dozens of victims of a 1920s epidemic of sleeping sickness. In each case, the person was "switched off" from real living. Apathetic, dull and listless are terms which were used to describe these patients' behavior. Through the administration of a new drug, L dopa, each of these patients showed a remarkable transformation. Almost like Rip Van Winkle, they woke from their sleep, and returned to life. Symptoms entirely disappeared. And for the first time in decades some of them once again became animated. My next few visits of Mrs. L. affirmed (in a most unexpected way), the power of music and just the right song to move the spirit into a new awakening.

Mrs. L. had spent many years in a local nursing home, and

in recent months was added to the names of those in hospice. I was asked to play music for her and distinctly remember the very first time that I had a chance to visit her. By the time I arrived in the late morning she was always seated in a small common room. Her eyes were sometimes open but mostly closed when I came to sing for her. I played a variety of songs, some with a more rhythmic beat to see if I could solicit a reaction out of her. I watched her face, her arms and her legs and feet. But alas, there was virtually no reaction. No facial expressions, no movement of the head, hands or feet. It was likely I was playing for some who was not there. I had learned that she had been like this for literally years, and that the nurses and social worker thought that perhaps music could help bring her out of her stupor. I was also told that she had gone blind many years ago, although it was believed that she still had the ability to hear. I spoke to her between songs, told her about myself in the hope that miraculously somehow, she would begin to answer and speak to me. However, this was not to be.

For the next five months or so I would visit Mrs. L. in the late morning. There she was, in the chair, with her eyes closed, simply sitting there with no communication and no one around her to try to stimulate her. But I will always remember my visit to Mrs. L on this day because things were about to significantly change. About fifteen minutes into my singing songs to her I decided to sing her the French song "Frere Jacques" for no other reason than I thought it might be a familiar song to her from her childhood that might bring back a childhood memory. And so, I began to sing:

> "Frere Jacques, frère Jacques, dormez-vous
>   dormez-vous
> Sonnez les matines sonnez les matines, ding ding
>   dong

Are you sleeping, are you sleeping, brother John, brother John?"

Out of the clear blue, after I sing "are you sleeping", Mrs. L. shouts out "No I'm not."

There was an aide nearby who also heard Mrs. L. speak for the first time in many months. I then began to sing the song all over again, and when I got to "are you sleeping" I asked her: "Are you sleeping?" And again, she responded: "No I'm not." From that moment on every time I would sing that song to her, she would respond. When I asked her if she was hungry, she replied: "I'm thirsty."

I continued my visits to Mrs. L. and each and every time, of course, I included Frere Jacques in my repertoire of songs. That one song had opened a portal of her brain that freed her to speak and have some meaningful conversation. It was as if the song awakened her. As a rabbi, I have always appreciated and admired the prayer in the Friday evening worship service that begins "Help us, our Father, to lie down I peace, and awaken us to life again our King." I have often found this concept of awakening to be one which I have experienced in both the educational and spiritual realm. Examples of the spiritual awakenings abound in the Bible. When Jacob was escaping the wrath of his brother Esau after he had stolen his birthright, he heads toward Haran. As night draws near, and he grows tired, Jacob pulls up a rock and puts it under his head and goes to sleep under the desert sky. As he sleeps, he dreams of a ladder with angels ascending and descending on it. When he finally awakens, he says: "Surely God is in this place, but I did not know." My colleague Rabbi Lawrence Kushner interprets Jacob's experience in modern language. He asked how could God be everywhere, and Jacob did not notice it? He answered with the following translation of that same verse: "Wow, God was really here, and I was out to lunch. I was sleeping. I missed it. Something awesome and extraordinary was happening around me and I was what the kids called OTL – out to lunch." In other words, God was here, but Jacob did not notice it because he wasn't fully present. His mind was somewhere else.

A similar example is that of Moses, when God says, "Come up to the mountain and be there." Why did God say, "be there?" Because he did not want Moses' head to be somewhere else. The basic idea of going up to a mountain is to be there when you get there. How many times do we try to get somewhere, and we are not there? Just like Sachs' victims of sleeping sickness, we are often in another world. God is all around us and yet we do not know it."

My visit to Mrs. L. was a wakeup call for me to appreciate the daily miracles of life itself. We should remember to be more mindful of the beauty of life itself, open our eyes to its beauty, and try to be there for someone in their time of need. The miracle of L dopa switched ill people into life. Singing just the right song helped open Mrs. L. to be able to speak again. May Mrs. L's memory serves as a blessing. I am so grateful to have been able to sing for her and to have had her in my life.

All the News That's Fit to Print (New York Times)

CHAPTER 4

The Newspaper Lady

One of my memories of my days in rabbinical school while married and living in Manhattan was getting my hands on the Sunday New York Times on Saturday night! It was getting a head start on a paper that had lots to read and getting a leg up on the reading was extremely helpful. My wife started doing the Sunday Times cross word puzzle, and for more than 40 decades continues to do every day's cross word puzzle, which she finds so very enjoyable. Over the years local newspapers have gone out of business due to being able to get the news in a variety of other ways. Although one can get a newspaper online, I still find something special about having a newspaper with real paper in my hand when reading it. Michael Connelly once wrote that "a newspaper is the center of a community. It's one of the tent poles of the community, and that's not going to be replaced by websites and blogs." I tend to agree with him.

What I learned in my second year in my position of Chords of Comfort was how important having a newspaper was to all my patients. Most nursing homes and assisted living facilities can have a newspaper delivered directly to the residents' rooms. I remember one of my patients, who was a retired engineer who always had newspapers in his room. But what was most memorable was the fact that they were rarely ever read. Instead, they were piled up on the dresser of my patient one on top of the other, but never opened. I began to wonder why and concluded that having a newspaper was part of his daily routine before having to reside in a nursing home and that his family want to preserve some semblance of being at home by providing him with his daily paper.

In year two I was asked to play for a Mrs. E. who resided in a local nursing home not far from my home. She was able to communicate somewhat with me, but what most intrigued me was the fact that she always had a newspaper in her hand when I arrived. And so, I would always begin my time with her asking "what's new in the world and in the paper?" What she often had to answer me was rather unintelligible, and yet nevertheless I persisted in talking about some of the things that were happening that day based on my perusing of the front page of the paper that she was holding in her hand. She really seemed to enjoy this. She also had several newspapers tucked into a compartment attached to a strap on the back of her wheelchair. All the papers were never opened and looked as if they had just been delivered. Some of them were over a week ago.

Between the many songs that I sang for her each time were conversations about places that she had visited with her family. Many of the stories that she was telling me were as if they were happening in the present. When I mentioned to her that I spend a couple of weekends a month in Wildwood New

Jersey she said to me that she was just there this past week. When I asked her what she was doing there Mrs. E. came up with all kinds of remarkably interesting stories. It gave her much pleasure to converse with me, and an opportunity for her to imagine what it would be like to leave the confines of the nursing home in which she found herself and go out into the world.

As the weeks passed and she became more and more comfortable with my visits she participated to a greater extent in my singing. Each and every time I came to visit the local New Jersey paper was in her hand and we began our time together by my asking her to tell me what she was reading that interested her and whether she could share some of her interests with me. I was told by the nurses that she got very few visits from friends and family and felt lonely a great deal of the time. So, my visiting her became a highlight of her week. She enjoyed the songs and she enjoyed our conversation, and she enjoyed telling me about her travels and her ability to be liberated from her surroundings.

The brain is an amazing mechanism. About the size of a half of grapefruit, it is capable of recording hundreds of memories per seconds for many decades without exhausting itself. It is the storehouse for billions of pieces and retains most everything it takes in and never forgets anything. Many pieces of information as the years go by are on permanent file in our brain. I learned that part of my work was to help my patients recall some of those things in their lives that will give them pleasure and comfort. It could be a song that they learned in early childhood and loved to sing, or it could be a family trip which they so much enjoyed and sometimes in their minds believe that they are taking the trip in the now all over again.

I have read that working on crossword puzzles (many

newspapers still feature them) can enhance one's memory power. Solving a crossword puzzle is a great way to exercise the brain and keep memory sharp. Research has even shown that doing a puzzle can help in keeping a variety of memory-related neurological illnesses in check. I never did get to know whether Mrs. E. was a cross word puzzle solver in her earlier years. Having her newspapers in hand though, definitely made her feel that each and every day she was enjoying a routine that was part of her daily life when living in her own home. For Mrs. E it was all the news that's fit to print.

Words are singularly the most powerful
force available to humanity

CHAPTER 5

The Word Puzzle Lady

*A*s a youngster I always enjoyed playing games. In my teen years I became fascinated with game shows on television and imagined myself one day as a contestant. The closest I ever got was Let's Make a Deal in Disneyworld which was an incredible amount of fun. While in Rabbinical school I pursued a doctorate at Teacher's College Columbia University. My dissertation was a study using games to teach Hebrew language comprehension. My dissertation confirmed that students had a lot more fun learning Hebrew while playing educational games. There are a multitude of word games on the market and in television. Wheel of Fortune, dubbed "America's Game" has been on television for decades. It is based on the old hang man game where players try to guess phrases while calling letters one at a time.

I was soon to be introduced to the word play lady, and

in addition to playing and singing for her I had a chance to watch her in action as she solved puzzles in which she tried to find hidden words.

When I first met Mrs. L. for the first time, she was in her room finishing her breakfast. I introduced myself and told her that I had come to play some music for her. She seemed pleased to have a visit and smiled as I held my guitar in hand and was soon to sing her my first song. I noticed on her table next to her food that there was a pile of what appeared to be magazines. As I looked more closely, I saw that all of them were word search books

A word search, word find, word seek, word sleuth or mystery word puzzle is a word game that consists of the letters of words placed in a grid, which usually has a rectangular or square shape. The objective of this puzzle is to find and mark all the words hidden inside the box. The words may be placed horizontally vertically, or diagonally. Often a list of the hidden words is provided, but more challenging puzzles may not provide a list. Many word search puzzles have a theme to which all the hidden words are related such as food, animals or colors.

After finishing her breakfast and after I had a chance to sing her a couple of songs (she smiled and applauded after each song but did not converse with me) she took the top magazine from the pile, opened to where she had left off, and promptly began to search for the hidden words (a list of the words were provided in her book). She was very persistent and carefully perused the entire grid with her eyes and her pencil until she finally lighted upon the word for which she was searching. When she put a pencil mark around the word she smiled, and I applauded and sang her a victory song.

She continued to move on to searching for all the words in the grid throughout our session together. On occasion she would get stuck and literally could not find the word which was disconcerting to her. After a while it was quite apparent that she was getting frustrated and I then decided that I was going to help her. Admittedly it took me a while to find the word she was looking for, but I too felt a moment of accomplishment and she was pleased too.

By the time I realized that our time had passed and that I had to go to visit my next patient Mrs. L. had finished the entire grid. There were more smiles and it was evident that this game was to help her fill her day with something meaningful that she enjoyed doing. And so, I wondered how often she had been doing word search puzzles and when it all started.

Over the course of the next several months I continued to sing and play for Mrs. L. Each time I arrived thereafter she was awake in her chair by her little desk, working on one of her word puzzle grids. I have now come to learn that although my purpose in visiting each patient is to use music for nourishment of the mind, body and soul, that each person has a talent or a passion which can continue to be honed with a little encouragement.

I became more and more fascinated with word search puzzles and began to study the research on them. I learned that word search puzzles emphasize pattern recognition, a key cognitive tool. A 2007 Harvard Business Review article (Gilkey and Kilts) discusses the benefits of puzzle solving to develop our skill at pattern recognition. There is also a Dopamine connection to word search puzzles. Dopamine is naturally produced in our brains. Touted as the "reward molecule," neuroscientists are linking dopamine to perseverance and the sense of accomplishment. When we finish a task, like finding words in a word search puzzle, our brains reward us with a surge of dopamine. Keeping this dopamine flowing can keep us motivated in other areas of our lives.

The combination of music therapy and word search was a winning formula for Mrs. L. She loved the music and she enjoyed working on her puzzles. And so, she will always be remembered by me as the Word Puzzle Lady.

Year Three

(Broadening Horizons)

Rock of Ages, let our song, praise Thy saving power. (Hanukkah hymn)

CHAPTER 1

Rock of Ages

I was now beginning my third year as Chords of Comfort and felt so much more comfortable with my daily routine and my ability to relate to a diverse group of patients with many health challenges. My work energized me knowing that each day would bring the possibility of lifting a person's spirits. When I would come back home each day, I would share with my wife the stories of that day. As a rabbi whose work involved pastoral care throughout my forty-year career I strongly feel that serving as a bedside musician for people in hospice is perhaps my most fulfilling work.

Although I am working for a Jewish hospice that is headed by a rabbi who is its chaplain, my patients are products of many faiths. For a Jewish patient it was helpful to me to be able to sing songs in Hebrew and Yiddish and even some prayers which they often asked me to sing. And when I played at a time such as Hanukkah, I would remind them of the holiday and sing Hanukkah songs that they loved and obviously recalled from their childhood. For those patients of the Christian faith, I prepared several Christmas carols (I learned many of these songs when in my High School choir back home in Toronto). I even translated Jingle Bells into Hebrew and would sing it to some of my non-Jewish patients.

During my visits at one nursing home I would often encounter Sister Ann. I met her for the first time when she was tending to a Catholic family of one of my patients who was transitioning and uncommunicative. I entered the room and Sister Ann was praying with the family. After she finished her prayers, I introduced myself as Chords of Comfort. I told them a little about myself and that I had come to play music for their loved one. Both the Sister and the family welcomed my presence and as it was the Christmas season, I played a couple of tranquil songs – Silent Night and O Little Town of Bethlehem. Everyone joined in the singing. How amazing – a rabbi in a room with a Holy Sister and a Catholic family singing Christmas carols. I stayed and played a few more songs and felt like my being present and offering my guitar and song was supportive to both my patient and her entire family.

A week later I again returned to the same nursing home, with several tambourines in a bag and my guitar strapped over my shoulder. It was then that I happened to run into the Sister who told me that in a few minutes she would be leading her weekly Mass in the chapel. (I had no idea that there was this beautiful chapel in the nursing home). When I asked whether I could observe since I had been told in advance that my patient for this visit was Catholic and might well wish to attend the Mass, Sister Ann was pleased to invite me in.

My patient for whom I sang for only a few short minutes was wheeled into the Chapel by the hospice aide. The Sister was already present, standing at the lectern with a large statue of the Virgin Mary standing next to her. She began to sing one of the prayers in the hymnal – some of the people in the room were able to communicate and sing along. Others were sitting there with head slumped and apparently sleeping. It was then that Sister Ann asked whether I could lead the group in the singing of "Rock of Ages." I did not immediately say yes, since I was not sure whether it was the only Rock of Ages that I knew in Hebrew which Jewish people sing at Hanukkah time, called Maoz Tzur. Turns out that this was a different Rock of Ages – other words and another melody. I told Sister Ann to begin singing it and I would accompany her and the rest of the people on guitar. The song went over well, and I felt so incredibly pleased to have participated in some way in my very first Mass. (Never could imagine this happening to me.)

I spontaneously had the idea that I would pass around tambourines to those in the chapel and offer another song that used hand motions. I asked Sister Ann whether this would be possible, and she immediately agreed to give it a try. I have a colleague who serves a congregation of hearing-impaired people, and he taught me some of the hand signs for the visually impaired, including the unique way that the word "halleluyah" – praise God – is signed. The way it is done is holding upward the index fingers of both hands and moving them upward in a spiral fashion as if lifting the words to the heavens.

The psalm that I would sing with the group was one of my favorites, Psalm 150 – the music psalm. It ends with the words "let everything that has breath praise God, halleluyah." This psalm was one of ten psalms that the Hasidic master Rabbi Nachman of Breslov identified as having special power to bring a true and complete healing. It may require a psycho-spiritual tour de force to praise God with happiness in the midst of illness, but Rabbi Nachman challenges us to do so.

Psalm 150 is a symphony of trumpet blasts, harp, lyre, timbrel, dance, lute, and cymbals. It ends with the line "let everything that has breath praise God, halleluyah." "Yah" is the breathiest name of God that is used in this Psalm which is a reminder that as long as we are able to breathe, we should praise and thank God for our lives.

With a brief introduction to the worshipers in attendance as to what we were going to do, I proceeded to teach them the melody to this beautiful song. Tambourines were shaken and many of the residents (including Sister Ann) raised their palms and index fingers. There was lots of engagement and I literally felt the very presence of God in the room at this time. Sister Ann had a huge smile on her face and loved every minute of the singing.

I told her that I had written an original melody to a song I titled "Let there be Peace, let there be Shalom in the whole wide world." I taught the Sister and the group how to sign the Hebrew word for peace – shalom. All one must do is hold up both palms of one's hand touching each other and making a complete circle using the hands. The idea here is that the Hebrew word "shalom" literally means completeness and wholeness, which is indicated by the perfect geometric figure, the circle. Mass ended with the words "let there be peace, let there be peace, in the whole wide world – "shalom, shalom…"

My day this day was now complete. I had a chance to offer my song to an entire group, including my patient in a chapel during a Mass. My spirits were buoyed, and I felt a wholeness unlike any before. For me, this experience was transformative. It offered me a chance to sing my songs in a holy setting with a warm and giving Sister. Psalm 133:1 summed up my feelings:

"How good it is for all brothers and sisters to dwell together in unity." That day we were all together in harmony.

*The whole world is a narrow bridge. The essence is
not to be afraid. (Rabbi Nachman of Breslov)*

CHAPTER TWO

Catholic TV

I was still riding high having had an opportunity to use my
music at a Mass. I have had the opportunity in my rabbinic
career of sharing a Thanksgiving eve service for many years
with a Methodist Church and I have always enjoyed my
interfaith work and bringing people together of different
backgrounds. Some church members have studied Bible
with me in my courses at my synagogue and I have had the
opportunity to teach Bible at the Church. Today I was going
to be meeting with a new patient who I was told especially
enjoyed Frank Sinatra songs. I prepared my playlist of songs,
studied the words and headed out to an assisted living to visit
a new patient.

Upon my arrival I took the elevator to the second floor and
knocked on the door of my patient. Upon arrival a woman
answered the door and was surprised to have a visitor early

in the morning. The woman (Mrs. D.) was the room mate of my patient, Mrs. G. She shared a beautiful apartment with Mrs. G. I introduced myself and told her that I had come to play some Frank Sinatra music. Mrs. D. said that it was not a good time, and would I be able to come back later that day. She said she and her roommate were watching an important television show, and that they preferred not to have it interrupted. Having other commitments, I asked whether I could come in and stay for a very few minutes to sing my songs after the television program ended. She acquiesced and ushered me in. She had me sit on the sofa and introduced me to Mrs. G. And then I turned my attention to the television show and watched with them.

To my great surprise, they were both watching Catholic TV which was airing a live church Mass that was being live streamed. I have enjoyed watching the Jewish Broadcasting Service programming which also streams each week a live Friday evening Sabbath service. I was unaware that Catholic TV did basically the same thing for those of the Christian faith. I had never attended a Church Mass so this would be my opportunity to watch the interaction between the priest and the two women in the room, and learn about the customs, rituals and traditions of a Mass.

The priest was very charismatic, and the singing was very lively. Mrs. G. and Mrs. D were fully engaged in the service and watching them in action reminded me of praying with one's whole heart and soul. It was embodied prayer at its very finest. Both Mrs. G. and Mrs. D. were so focused on the service that they totally forgot that I was even present in the room. I could see from their facial signs and rhythmic movements of their arms how engrossed they were with the prayer service. I watched as they made the sign of the cross.

When it ended and the priest signed off, they turned

the television off and asked whether I enjoyed watching too. I told them that I had never observed a Mass before and asked whether it would be all right if I could ask them some questions about what I witnessed. I inquired about the altar with its linens, the chalice, the candles, the priest's vestments, the flowers and the purpose of the incense. The two women were eager to explain all of these to me and how each of these items helps to impart the Church's teachings. I had one of the best comparative religion classes ever. It was experiential learning at its best. It was as if I had been on a field trip to church with parishioners and afterward had an opportunity to ask questions.

Looking at my watch I realized that I had only a small window of time before I had to visit my next patient. I told Mrs. G. that I could stay for only a few more minutes and was told that she enjoyed Frank Sinatra songs. She was surprised that I knew all this information about her (I got an advance from her hospice social worker). And so, I took my guitar in hand and started to sing the Frank Sinatra rendition of New York New York:

> *Start spreading the news*
> *I am leaving today*
> *I want to be a part of it*
> *New York, New York*
>
> *I want to wake up in that city*
> *That doesn't sleep*
> *And find I'm king of the hill*
> *Top of the heap....*

This morning I was feeling like the king of the hill. And as the New York New York song says near its end: "If I can make it there, I'll make it anywhere." It was an extraordinarily successful pastoral visit and I truly felt that I made it there. And yes, I told my two ladies that I would like to come back and visit next week and wanted to be sure that I would not be interrupting their Catholic TV mass. They told me a day and time that would work, and the following week I was able to play an array of Sinatra songs. The engagement was positive, with a lot of singing along and participation.

Every canvas is a journey all its own (Pablo Picasso)

CHAPTER THREE

Painting Classes

In addition to nurses, doctors, aides, cooks, hairdressers and the like, each nursing home also staffs a recreation director. This person is responsible for designing the activities of the day, so that patients that are able can interact with other patients and have the stimulation of visual and physical activity. Often arriving at a nursing home, I have witnessed patients bowling with plastic balls and pins, playing trivia games, playing card games, playing bingo, singing karaoke, passing and hitting balloons, pet visits, and chair yoga. Therapeutic recreation provides the opportunity for new experiences and helps residents find creative ways to continue old interests that might be challenging due to disabilities. Activities also foster socialization with peers. There is a theory that when we are depressed, we stop doing the things we enjoy, thus leading to depression. In order to become less depressed, we need to engage in activities we used to find pleasurable, even if we do not feel like it. Once we do something fun, it energizes us enough to take the next pleasant action.

Nursing home patients no longer have to cook, clean or take care of chores. When life's tasks no longer take the bulk of the day, it is essential to fill the time with something else constructive. Therapeutic recreation provides the opportunity for new experiences and helps residents find creative ways to continue old interests that might be challenging due to disabilities. Activities that encourage residents to speak up such as trivia or group reminiscence are unbelievably valuable. I have come to learn in my experience as Chords of Comfort that a good recreation department gives residents the opportunity to create a new life.

One of my favorite patients in my third year of Chords of Comfort was a retired engineer. Mr. S. so much enjoyed telling me all about his work as an engineer, the pictures on his wall in his room, his joy of reading the newspaper. He enjoyed singing along to all my songs. I taught him hand signing and he loved using his arms and hands to spiritual songs. It was my version of prayer aerobics. He also enjoyed using the tambourine that I gave him each time I visited. He would tap to the beat of the song and was totally engrossed in the song and its rhythm. At first, I wondered what he was even doing in a nursing home. After some time in our conversation he began to leave the world of reality and talk about things as if they were there, but they were not. On one occasion when visiting him I found him in the common room with the recreational director who was playing a game of poker with the residents. Residents would win candy and really enjoyed the game and the action.

One of my fondest memories of visiting Mr. S. is when I went to play for him and was told that he was in the activity room of the nursing home. I went to the activity and there he was, seated at a table with many other residents. The art

therapist then proceeded to offer a show and tell on the painting of some of the great masterpiece artists. It was a beautifully
presented visual presentation and I learned a great deal about
the art and lives of some of the great master paintings. After
her presentation the aides presented each resident with two
colors of paint and two brushes, and each was given a small
piece of cardboard (each in a different shape) upon which
were various spaces in which to paint within the lines either
using one or the other color that was provided for them. I
went to sit next to Mr. S. and he barely said hello. He was very
intent on getting his painting completed in a timely fashion
and enjoyed the process very much. In fact, all the residents
were actively engaged in the project and I too became engaged
in watching all the action very intently. I hummed some tunes
while he was doing his painting which he seemed to enjoy.
Aides went around the various tables making sure that the
colors were painted on the cardboard in the proper way. Mr. S.
finished his project and when I looked at it I could not for the
life of me determine what the picture was. In fact, no image
came to my mind when I looked at it. I walked around to the
other patients and their paintings too in various other colors
had no recognizable image.

I then thought to myself that the objective of the painting
therapy was to simply paint colors between the lines which I
know can be very therapeutic. But next came the big surprise.
One by one each person was asked to bring his or her small
picture to the front of the room. An easel stand was set up
upon which was placed a large foam board. The art therapist
took each of the smaller paintings that were made by the
residents, and one by one appended them to the easel. I now
became more intrigued since it now appeared that each resident had painted part of puzzle that when put together would
reveal a picture. When all the pieces had been placed onto the

foam board it revealed a lovely picture of Marilyn Monroe! And then the art therapist asked if anyone could identify her. A couple of hands went up and were successful in the identification. And then the art therapist congratulated everyone for creating their masterpiece. It was a masterful lesson that had me fully engaged. Seeing the picture of Marilyn being revealed was worth a thousand words. It was truly a masterpiece.

I asked the therapist whether she would mind if I sang everyone a song before they went to lunch. She was pleased to afford me the opportunity and I sang a song that most everyone in the room knew – This land is your land. Most everyone joined with me in the song. It was a glorious day.

I will sing to the Lord all my life (Psalm 104:33)

Singing the Bible

On a wintry midweek morning I headed over to a nursing home with which I was familiar. It is a Jewish nursing home that has its own rabbi/chaplain, offers a Sabbath worship service each week and serves kosher food. During my years of service as a congregational rabbi I would bring the students of my teen Hebrew High School on a pre-Passover field trip. In advance students prepared various presentations using their talents. We had dancers, comedians, magicians and acrobats. The goal was to put on a performance before Passover that we called The Matzah Ball. When arriving at the nursing home each student was asked to partner with a resident, introduce themselves and get acquainted. The show began with me playing a couple of familiar sing-along songs on my guitar and then the full Matzah Ball show began with the various acts. We finished the show inviting those residents who were able to join in dancing a hora to the tune of "Hava

Nagila." It was a magical evening enjoyed by residents and students alike.

This morning, I was asked to play for a Mrs. P. When I entered her room the first thing I noticed was all the biblical art on the walls. There were verses from the Book of Isaiah – Arise and shine; The Lord is my Shepherd I shall not want; Praise the Lord with the timbrel and harp. There was a crucifix appended to the wall and a picture of Jesus. It was immediately apparent to me that Mrs. P. was likely a woman whose faith was especially important to her. I also noticed a large well used Bible sitting on her nightstand. I introduced myself to Mrs. P. and helped her as she was finishing her breakfast. She was extremely cordial and appreciative of my help. I told her a little about myself and my background, and she told me about her family and children who often visit on weekends. When I asked her whether she would like to have me play some music for her she immediately gave me the two thumbs up.

Knowing that the Bible resonated with her I went on to play my first tune, based on Psalm 150:

Halleluyah, praise God in His sanctuary, for His power
    praise Him
Praise Him with trumpet calls
With harp and lyre praise him.
Praise Him with drum and dance
With flute and strings praise Him.
Praise him with clashing cymbals
Let every breath of Life praise the Lord, halleluyah.

I know a lovely tune using the word "halleluyah" and when we reached the end of the Psalm and I sang it, she joined along with me. She had a beautiful voice and loved to sing. We had a brief conversation in which I asked her to tell me about some of her favorite Prophets. When she told me she liked Isaiah, I sang her Isaiah's vision "nation shall not lift up sword against nation, neither shall people learn war anymore. When I finished the song, she shouted "Amen!"

I then asked Mrs. P. whether she could tell me something about her Bible, which based on its condition looked very well used. She said it was a family Bible that she reads each and every day. I asked her whether she would like me to read to her something from the Bible and she said "of course." I began to read Psalm 23 "The Lord is My Shepherd, I shall not want." Without me having to say another word she proceeded to recite the entire prayer by memory: "He makes me to lie down in green pastures, he leads me beside the still waters.' It was a powerful moment for me, since Psalm 23 is a Psalm of comfort reminding us that one need not fear death, because God is always with us.

For centuries Jews and others have turned to the Book of Psalms for solace, guidance, and much more. Psalms pervade the established Jewish daily liturgy, and Jewish tradition has encouraged people to turn to them when needed for support. The Levites sang the psalms in the ancient Temple and the Jewish Sabbath service is filled with them. For my next two Psalms I chose ones that I have considered Jewish healing songs because of their evocative words. And so, I sang to her "Have hope in the Lord, be strong and your heart will be strengthened" (Psalm 27:143) and "I will lift up my eyes to the mountains: Where will my help come from? My help comes from the Lord, Creator of Heaven and earth." (Psalm 121:1–2)

As our time together was winding down one of the volunteers that visits patients entered the room with his Bible in hand. He had come prepared to read Mrs. P. more biblical passages. I asked him whether he would join with me in one final song/prayer which is sung every day in the Jewish liturgy. It is one of the prayers par excellence for peace. We sang it together as Mrs. P. listened intently: *May the One who brings peace to the universe bring peace to us and to all who dwell on earth.* I bid Mrs. P. adieu, wished her God's blessings and shouted one final "halleluyah" to which she responded Praise the Lord! Amen.

Only a life lived in the service of others
is worth living. (Albert Einstein)

CHAPTER 5
Mr. Mayor

*I*n addition to my work as Chords of Comfort I am currently the rabbi of the only synagogue in Cape May County. One of its members is a Deputy Mayor and I have been asked to offer a prayer on special occasions such as at 9/11 Memorial Services. In Central New Jersey I was congregational rabbi of the only synagogue in my town. As such the Mayor of our town would often call upon me to offer a message or prayer at a civic event. I commended him for his outstanding service to our community, wondering how he was able to do it all since his day job was a High School Science teacher. He said that he wanted to serve his community.

In Judaism the concept of community is an especially important one. It is no accident that the Jewish people called themselves "the people of Israel." A sense of peoplehood has long been the defining characteristic of the Jewish people,

Wherever Jews have lived, they have built synagogues and established communal organizations and created systems of communal governance. The most famous verse in Jewish tradition which emphasizes the interconnectedness of the individual and the community is that of Rabbi Hillel who in the Ethics of the Fathers (1:14) said: If I am not for myself, who is for me? And if I am only for myself, what am I?"

One of my last patients in my fourth year serving in my role as Chords of Comfort was a man who I was told by the hospice people was a former Mayor of a neighboring town. I had never played for a Mr. Mayor before and was excited to meet him and learn about his life. It took several calls to his home for us to come up with an agreeable time to meet at his home. When I arrived, I was soon to learn that it would take quite a while before I could even consider singing my songs.

When I arrived, he ushered me in and had me sat down at his dining room table. There on the table was a huge box of papers and I imagined that they were filled with articles about his work as Mayor of the city some three decades ago. After introducing himself he asked me whether I would like to learn a little about the local town. Not wanting to disappoint him I said "certainly." It was then that he began to tell me the story of his birth when the town was just three years old, and how it had changed over the years. When I asked Mr. Mayor to tell me what was in the box he began by pulling out a piece of paper that literally was a story of the summary of his life – when and where he was born, where he went to school, where he was employed, his service in the Korean war, and his nine years as Mayor.

Mr. Mayor told me that his interest in government came about by the example shown to him by his parents. They were so proud that they were Americans and were able to vote.

Youngest of six children, his father traveled first to the United States, but it took a while for his mother and oldest sister to arrive from Italy because of World War II. His father joined the U.S Army, became an American citizen and after saving enough money he settled in his town. And at age 37 he came his town's youngest Mayor. I thought it was important for him to tell me the story of his life after which he took out of the box a variety of newspaper clippings which featured him in stories about the town and his mayoral accomplishments. He was so enormously proud to share with me his many challenges and successes as mayor.

This day I felt that less music and more listening would be beneficial. And so, I listened to his reminiscences about his time in local government as well as listening to some of his health concerns. I felt enriched and empowered in visiting him and felt that the benefit of raising his spirits not only flowed to him but also to me, the visitor. It was as if I asked Mr. Mayor 'Give me your hand' and it was I who rose up stronger and straighter because of the touch. It was toward the end of our conversation that he finally asked to hear me play a couple of my songs.

He had spent some time telling me about his many visits to see the Brooklyn Dodgers play as he sat in the bleachers. And so, I played, and we sang together "Take Me Out to the Ballgame."

Just before I was about to leave, he asked me one more thing. "Would you like to see my sports memorabilia?" I really needed to go on with my other visits that day but decided a few more minutes with him would be time well spent. And I, too was a baseball memorabilia collector and honestly was interested in what he might have to show me. Given that his memories were all in a box and not very well kept, I was expecting the same with his baseball cards.

To my surprise he left the room to get his collection and came back with a binder which I was not expecting And then when he opened it up it revealed an almost complete set of baseball cards in pristine condition from 1956 which included many of my childhood heroes. He also had a substantial collection of autographed baseballs. I perused his collection and commended him on the condition of his memorabilia. And as I was leaving, I asked him to join me in one more round of "Take Me Out to the Ballgame."

Year Four

(Building Relationships)

*In remembrance lies the secret of
redemption (Baal Shem Tov)*

CHAPTER ONE

My First Memorial Service

M emory has always been a part of the Jewish tradition. Throughout the Bible the Israelites are commanded to remember that they were strangers in the land of Egypt, and once freed have the obligation to assist the orphan and widow. The Bible (Leviticus 19:9:9) instructs us to leave a portion of one's harvest behind for the poor and the stranger. Passover is the time that Jews remember, during their Passover seder, the time that they were freed from Egypt and are furthermore told that they should feel as if they were freed from slavery in Egypt. And when one loses a loved one there are special times throughout the year when Jews remember their loved ones by reciting special memorial prayers and lighting a candle in their memory

Ironically, there is a special wing in many nursing homes
called the Memory unit. It is in this wing that you find many
of the people with dementia who have lost most of their
memory. I have had an opportunity to play music for many
people in the memory unit and have personally witnessed the
sadness of a spouse who has come to visit his wife who has
no recollection as to who her husband is. Now in my fourth
year as Chords of Comfort I began playing music for a lovely
couple in an assisted living facility. Mr. and Mrs. B. loved to
have me come and sing my songs for them. They offered me
some juice and cookies every time that I came to play for them,
which was over the course of quite several months. Sadly, Mrs.
B. died and shortly thereafter Mr. B's health began to decline,
and he was moved to the nursing wing next to the assisted
living facility.

Two weeks after his wife's passing, I was asked again to
play music for Mr. B. Upon arrival he was laying in his bed
and immediately recognized me when I walked into his room,
addressing me as rabbi. Several of his children were also
present that day and I introduced myself to them. There was an
exceptionally large photo of a smiling Mrs. B. hung on the wall
in his room which he could see from his bedside. His voice
now was much weaker, and I offered my condolences upon
the loss of his wife. I played several tranquil songs including a
healing psalm and Mr. B spoke about his wonderful wife and
children. He was heartbroken that he had lost his beloved
loving companion and I told him how I honored I was to
have met her acquaintance. In a subdued voice he told me
how much he loved her and missed her.

I came to visit Mr. B. several more times and each time
when I arrived, he smiled when I walked into the room,
addressing me as rabbi. The large picture of his smiling wife

was on the wall and seemed to be staring directly at him. It was a way of keeping her memory with him in the room. His condition was weakening and after only a couple of songs he closed his eyes and went to sleep. I continued to sit by his bedside and hummed a couple of quiet songs. I bid him God's blessings and was off to see my next patient.

That week I received an e mail from the hospice social worker telling me the family of Mr. B. asked whether it would be possible for me to conduct a Memorial service at the nursing home in his room. Not knowing exactly what the family was looking for I decided to contact them and discuss their idea. They were interested in a brief service that would include some song, the Jewish prayer which petitions God to rest a soul in peace and an opportunity at the end for the family to recite the Kaddish, the Mourner's Prayer. I was more than pleased to oblige them, and we set a time for the Memorial service.

I was very touched that the family wanted to have this opportunity for Mr. B to be able to memorialize his wife in song and prayer. And that they had chosen me was an honor. I arrived on a Thursday morning and the family was in the room. I noticed that they had prepared some food and beverage to be served following the memorial service. (It is customary following a Jewish burial that the family return to the home of the deceased for what is called the meal of condolence). Mr. B was pleased to meet me, and I began the Memorial service with the recitation of Psalm 23, known as the Psalm of comfort: "The Lord is my Shepherd, I shall not want…"

I then talked to the family about the things that are lasting in life, including the importance of having a good name and reputation. To the memory of Mrs. B. I read some rabbinic verses related to the crown of a good name:

There are three crowns, our Sages taught:
The crown of Torah, the crown of priesthood and the
*   crown of royalty*
But the crown of a good name excels them all.
A good name is to be treasured above previous oil
Wealth, like health may pass away
But a good name can live on forever.
Therefore, our ancient Sages taught:
The righteous need no monuments
Their good deeds are their memorials
The earth of the grave does not cover them
The hand of time does not erase them.
The kindness and love they have shown remain in
*   everlasting remembrance.*

I was now about to conclude the brief memorial service with the chanting of the traditional prayer known in Hebrew as *Eil Malei Rachamim*. This prayer is chanted in the synagogue on all the special days of remembrance on the Jewish calendar at the service known as Yizkor, Remembrance. And so I began to sing:

O God, filled with compassion, grant perfect peace in your sheltering presence to the soul of our beloved Mrs. B. We ask that you remember all of those worthy and kind deeds which she performed throughout her life. May her soul be given eternal life, and may her memory serve as a blessing to all those who knew and loved her. And may she rest everlastingly in peace.

To which the family responded: "Amen."

I decided that I was going to conclude the memorial service to the memory of Mrs. B. by asking the family to join me in the recitation of the Mourner's Kaddish. Interestingly the Kaddish prayer does not include a single syllable about death or immortality. Rather from beginning to end, the Kaddish sanctifies the name of God, thus affirming one's submission to and acceptance of God's will. Though sorrow may temporarily dull the vision of the bereaved and threaten to rob life of meaning, the Kaddish affirms that there is a plan and a purpose to life because there is a God at the heart of it. And so, the Kaddish praises God's name and reminds the bereaved that sorrow can help one to become more sympathetic to the hurt of others.

The Kaddish is usually recited while standing, and it was not my intention to ask Mr. B to get out of his bed and try to stand. However, he insisted, and with the help of his children he was lifted out of his bed. The family locked arms and so we began to recite the Kaddish:

> Yitgadal v'yitkadash shmey rabbah
> Magnified and sanctified by the Name of God
>   throughout the world...
> May God who ordains harmony in the universe grant
>   peace to us, to all Israel and to all who dwell on
>   earth.

The Kaddish prayer itself has acquired a quality of immortality. It is a gracious way to honor the dead and to ennoble the living. For Mr. B. and his family, the memorial service allowed for yet another opportunity to cherish memories of their loved one. I shall always remember my having the honor of remembering Mrs. B. in a service that allowed her beloved husband to participate, along with the immediate family. It was an opportunity to facilitate a tribute to this beloved and kind woman.

Our memories of loved ones continue to help shape us and

hopefully take what was best in their lives and use it for good in the world. Ours is an active existence. If we are fortunate enough to retain the gift of our memory, we should use it to help us in making the world a better place. And if we do so, we can help realize the words of the Baal Shem Tov which adorn the walls of Yad VaShem – the Holocaust Memorial Museum in Israel: "In remembrance lies the secret of redemption."

*"Dust you are and unto dust you
shall return" (Genesis 3:19)*

CHAPTER TWO

My First Almost
Communion

I had come to learn over the last few years that many of the
nursing homes and assisted livings that I have visited held
worship services for the residents. In one of the nursing homes
where many of my Chords of Comfort patients resided the
Catholic Mass was held on the third Tuesday of every month
in the late morning. I had already experienced two Catholic
Masses at this nursing home. At the most recent I made a visit
to a new patient on a Tuesday morning and by the time I had
arrived Mrs. S. was already in attendance at the Mass. Never
having met her I walked into the room where the service was
taking place and once again Sister Ann was conducting the pro-
ceedings. Apparently, the Priest who was there at the beginning
was making his rounds to offer Communion to others in the
nursing home who were unable to leave their rooms.

Sister Ann saw me as I seated myself and she was playing hymns on a tape recorder to which residents were joining in the singing. She said that she was expecting the priest to return shortly but on this day he had not returned. At that point Sister Ann turned to me and asked me whether I wished to take over saying that I surely must know some Christian songs. Thinking quickly, I thought of all those songs and prayers that Jews and Christians have in common. The Book of Psalms had some good ones, and so I agreed to lead the residents in some prayerful Psalms. Sister Ann introduced me as Rabbi Ron who was going to offer live music.

At that moment, an aide returned to the room and told Sister Ann that the priest would be longer than expected. I now realized that it was I who would be in charge of the Mass and its singing. I played and sang a version of Psalm 150 using the beautiful Halleluyah melody composed by Leonard Cohen. Everyone participated and it was a joyous celebration in song and praise.

Sister Ann loved it as well, and it was a sacred celebration. After the Mass concluded I spent some additional private time with Mrs. S. and sang a variety of songs for her.

I was given a new patient, Mr. D., and I recall that it was on a Wednesday morning that I headed over to the nursing home to visit him. This nursing home has a most beautiful worship chapel. Upon arrival I went to Mr. D's room. I peeked inside and saw that he was not there. There were many possibilities as to where he might be – the activities room, the hair salon, physical therapy, and the like. When I went to the nurses' station, I was told that he was with other residents at a prayer service in the chapel. I was now confused, since I had learned that this nursing home always holds its Mass on the third Tuesday of each month.

And so, I headed over to the chapel which was filled with

residents and some of their family members. There were also staff members present too and I was now wondering why this crowd was so large. I saw Mr. D. (noticing his name written on the back of his wheelchair) and some other familiar faces including several hospice aides. There was a priest and a person playing the piano and some people were holding small paper hymnal booklets. But why everyone was here on a Wednesday morning was still puzzling to me.

I asked one of the nurses sitting at the back of the chapel what the special occasion was on this day for this Mass. And then she told me that I had come on Ash Wednesday. I could not believe my good fortune since I had never witnessed an actual Ash Wednesday commemoration. I know that Ash Wednesday is one of the most popular and important holy days in the Christian liturgical calendar, opening the season of Lent, a season of fasting and prayer. Observed chiefly by Catholics, many other Christians observe it too. It appears that Ash Wednesday comes from the ancient Jewish tradition of penance and fasting. The practice includes the wearing of ashes on the head, symbolizing the dust from which God made us. And as the priest applies the ashes to a person's forehead, he speaks the words "Remember that you are dust, and to dust you shall return." The ashes are made from palm branches, taken from the previous year's Palm Sunday Mass. (Jews also use the palm on their festival of the harvest, known as Sukkot).

I followed the action during the worship service and observed the priests and his assistants administer communion to the residents and guests. I decided to take a couple of steps outside of the chapel in order not to have myself directly participate in the communion. But it was fascinating to watch the action for the very first time in my life.

Toward the end of the Mass I watched as the priest and his attendants began administering the ashes by placing them on the forehead of the residents. As they got to the back of the chapel one of those administering the ashes began to approach me. It looked as if I was going to get my forehead to be marked by ashes. (At that moment I thought of the Ninevites in the Book of Jonah story who did penance in sackcloth and ashes which ultimately led them to be saved because of their true and authentic repentance). Sister Ann who was standing near the back of the chapel noticed someone approaching me with the ashes, and at the last moment intervened and asked that I not be among the participants.

It was a moving worship service and my first time witnessing an Ash Wednesday. One of my favorite Bible verses is in the Book of Micah (6:8) which states: "He has told you O man what is good, and what the Lord requires of you: Do justly, love goodness and walk humbly with God. There is no doubt in my mind that this is the essence of being a good person, including the importance of staying humble. And that is one of the purposes of marking the forehead with ashes – to humble the heart and remind us that life passes away on Earth and that like Adam, we were made from the dust and shall eventually return to it.

And so, another day in my life as Chords of Comfort was soon to draw to an end. Even though I found myself in a room with a worship service that was not a part of my faith I left with a warm feeling in my heart and felt the spirituality of those in attendance. I appreciated the opportunity of witnessing firsthand this holy occasion. If more people would have the opportunity to spend time together with people of other faiths, I believe that it would enable strangers to be better neighbors in a global community.

Even in old age they shall bear fruit (Psalm 92)

CHAPTER 3
The 106-Year-Old Man

The life expectancy of Americans is longer than ever before. Between 1900 and 2000, the average life expectancy increased by nearly thirty years in the United States and most other developed countries of the world, and the developing world is catching up quickly. For the first time in history, people born can expect to live seven, eight, nine or more decades. Adults 60 and older are now the fastest growing segment of our population. The Jewish people from its outset has paid attention to the elderly. In many biblical passages the "elders" are the wise men, the judges of the people. We read in the Book of Leviticus (19:32) "You shall rise up before the hoary head and honor the face of the old man, and you shall fear the Lord."

The rabbis of bygone years understood this verse literally, that whenever an old person passes by one should rise to one's feet as a token of respect. On public buses in Israel this sign bearing the biblical verse appears asking people to offer their seat if a person climbs aboard a bus and would have difficulty standing during the ride.

My patient today was a man named Mr. R. who was living in an assisted living facility. I knocked on the door and there was no answer. I slowly pushed the door open and Mr. R. was seated on his wheelchair at the back of his room, facing the window. Entering the room there were some amazing paintings on the wall and an interesting letter on White House stationery wishing Mr. R. a happy birthday on his 100th birthday. The letter was signed "Barak and Michelle Obama." I now knew that I was visiting a centenarian which made the visit even more exciting. I went up to Mr. R. and introduced myself to him. He pointed to the ear with the hearing aid, indicating that I needed to speak loudly and clearly.

I told Mr. R. that I had come to play some music for him. He seemed pleased that someone had come to spend some time with him. I then asked him to tell me something about his life. Mr. R. was pleased to oblige and so began his life story, beginning when he was suffering from a debilitating illness at age 7 months in South Africa. I was now thinking and realizing that it would take more than one visit to hear his entire life's story.

Turns out that George is 106 years old, married to a woman who predeceased him by 30 years, and had no children. In his 106 years he witnessed the advent of the Empire State Building – going to the top the year it opened – homes with and without electricity, an internment camp, depressions and two World Wars. His family knew both Winston Churchill "not so nice" and Mahatma Gandhi "very nice." He had a 50-year marriage to his beloved wife but no children. He was immensely proud of his American citizenship, travels through-out the world and his almost 40 years of employment at the

Paper Company. He said that he still voted when elections came up and liked to go to the voting station in person rather than mail in ballot. By the time I finished singing him one or two songs it was time for him to go down to the dining room for lunch. I told him I would be back to see him, and he said that he looked forward to it. His handshake was quite firm, and I thought of how wonderful it was that he still has an appreciation and zest for life, and in addition is in possession of all his faculties.

The next time I came to visit Mr. R. he was already in the lunchroom in the middle of his meal, sitting at a table all by himself. The others had already finished eating and had left, but Mr. R. was very mindful of his food and ate slowly, chewing every morsel. I sat down at his table and took out my guitar and we sang several songs while he was eating. He said to me "that was very nice" with a beautiful sweet smile on his face. It was then that he began talking politics with me, telling me that he saw himself as a Republican but had voted democratic on occasion depending on who was running. Because he told me how proud he was when he finally became an American citizen, I sang to him America the Beautiful and he joined in singing it with me. It was a tender moment.

Before dessert was to be served, I wanted to ask him about how he felt to still be living at more than 100 years old. He said that he missed his wife very much and was rather lonely because he had outlived almost all his friends. However, he said that every day during the afternoon when the sun would come through his apartment window that he would sit facing the sunshine and take in the light of the day. He said this warmed his heart and made him feel better. And then I remember asking him to what he attributed his living to be more than 100. I could never have imagined his reply. He immediately responded: "I eat ice cream every day for lunch and dinner." I then asked him what flavors are served. He said usually just three-strawberry, vanilla and chocolate. I then responded that I enjoy eating ice cream too.

One more song and then someone in the kitchen brought out his dessert. It was a two-scoop dish of chocolate ice cream. There were other choices, but that's what he wanted to eat. He also asked whether I would like to join him, and another dish of ice cream was brought out and given to me. And there we were – the two of us enjoying the food promising a long life.

On the occasion of the 106th birthday of Mr. R. a New Jersey newspaper did a feature story on Mr. R. It was a great article with a beautiful picture of a smiling Mr. R. I remember cutting out the picture and the next time I visited him I asked whether he could autograph the picture for me to keep. He told me that he had a bit of arthritis in his writing hand and that his autograph would not be as good as when he was younger. He signed his picture with a very legible signature, and I keep a framed copy in my home office, so that when I look up from my computer a smiling Mr. R. is facing me.

I feel privileged to have met such an energetic and inter-esting man. Numerous times he thanked me with his broad smile for coming and offering him companionship. In Judaism attaining 120 years with undiminished abilities has come to be considered the ideal life span because according to the Bible Moses reached that age "with his eyes undimmed and his vigor unabated." (Deuteronomy 34:7) In Jewish tradition, the blessing of "120 years" is frequently offered to people on their birthdays.

Mr. R. passed away peacefully at age 107. I am reminded each day when I often think of him and look at his photo that we should appreciate the gift of life and be thankful each and every day for this most precious gift. Each visit with him reinforced my appreciation for the vitality, wisdom and life lessons that a senior citizen can offer. For me Mr. R. epitomizes the verse in Psalm 92:13–15:

> *The righteous bloom like a palm tree*
> *They thrive like a cedar in Lebanon …*
> *Even in old age they still bear fruit*
> *They are full of sap and freshness.*

Like Mr. R. I hope that we all will learn to number our days, remain optimistic and live our lives to the fullest. And as the saying goes, "till 120", and let's not forget the ice cream!

Music gives a soul to the universe, wings to the mind, flight to the imagination and life to everything. (Plato)

CHAPTER 4

Name That Tune

As my fourth year as Chords of Comfort moved into the fall, I was driving on my way to see a new patient residing in one of the nursing homes that I have been frequenting. Her name is Mrs. T. and I was told by the hospice people that she really enjoys singing and knows her music too. The first thing I remember about her is that when arriving quite early in the morning she was already up, dressed, had eaten, and was watching television in her room. This is not the norm. Many of many patients are not ready for my visit until the latter part of the morning and eat their breakfast when it is almost noon time.

Mrs. T. was very pleasant when I introduced myself for the first time. She was able to converse with ease, and just looking at her it was difficult to imagine that she was a hospice patient. When I asked her whether she liked music she responded with an enthusiastic "of course." She said that she liked "oldie songs" and just for the fun of it I sang Old MacDonald Had a Farm and had her sing all the sounds that the animals make along with me. The song seemed to resonate with her, and the animal sounds part of the song offered her a chance to be creative.

It was then that a new thought came to my mind to make my sing song into a game that she could play with me. I told her that for my next song I was not going to sing the words, but instead sing "la la la la" while playing guitar. I told her that she was then to try to guess the name of the song. I thought this would be a good motivational exercise that would get her brain to think more about the melody and the song. And so, I began with my first song, singing "la la la" to the melody of jingle bells.

I could see her facial expressions deep in thought as she listened attentively to the melody trying to figure it out. I appeared that she was trying to put words to the song when I saw her moving her lips. When I finished singing the song, I asked whether she could tell me what its name was. She said it sounded somewhat familiar, but she could not come up with the answer. I then asked whether she would like more time and have me sing it again. And so, the" la la la's" continued one more time until I finished all of the song. And then came the eureka moment when she blurted out "jingle bells." She was so enormously proud that she was able to guess the song without words.

I then asked whether she would like to continue playing the game and try another song. She was eager to try, and this time (without words) I sang Mary had a little lamb. She began to hum the song to herself and soon she was able to figure it out and shouted out "Mary had a little lamb." I then proceeded to sing the song again, only this time with the words. As one who had done research on using games for educational purposes in graduate school this music game that I was playing with Mrs. T. affirmed the research that many people enjoy playing games because of the challenge that it affords.

I did not want to make her too tired, so I sang a couple of songs to her with words simply for her pleasure and enjoyment. She applauded at the end of each song. As the weeks went on, I continued to visit Mrs. T. and play the guessing game that she played with me the first time we met. It was then that I suddenly remembered the popular game show on television "Name that Tune", when contestants were asked to name a song when only provided with the opening few notes of the song. Perhaps Mrs. T would be able to guess a song given only the first 5–7 notes, so on one occasion I prepared a couple of well-known songs to see if she could guess them with providing only the first few notes. She was able to successfully identify one of the songs, and I remember it as being Yankee Doodle.

Ever since primitive people learned to create musical sounds and instruments, instrumental music and song have carried special significance. The Bible is filled with the idea that it is natural for people to burst forth spontaneously into song when moved by the signs and wonders of God. King David was known as the "sweet singer of the Israel" and his many poems in the Book of Psalms have been set to melodies. I hope to continue to sing songs in my role of Chords of Comfort in the years to come. I cannot imagine a world without music. As Friedrich Nietzsche once wrote: "Without music, life would be a mistake."

*If every day is awakening, you will never grow
old. You will just keep growing. (Gail Sheehy)*

CHAPTER 5

Awakenings

*I*could never have imagined the opportunities that have
presented themselves to me because of my God-given voice
and being able to play music on my guitar. While serving
as a congregational rabbi I had many opportunities to lead
congregants in prayer (now with guitar in hand), singing for
the religious school student assemblies, and volunteering
to play for children and seniors at local Jewish community
Centers. I have used my music at interfaith services and during
my student years performed as a professional musician in a
well-known Hebrew folk rock group. My singing paid my
tuition!

But there is nothing that quite compares to the last four
years, when I have been privileged to visit nursing homes,
assisted living facilities and private homes to sing and play

music for people in hospice. On some days, my patients are alert and able to converse with me. On others, they lie in bed unable to communicate and sometimes sleep. On those occasions I sit by their bedside, sing quiet songs and keep them company. Sometimes a family member or two is present. I remember once learning that even in the womb a fetus can hear sounds, and that the last thing a person loses is sound. And so, I play, even when someone is sleeping.

Being present and ensuring that no one is left alone is an incredible act of kindness and a supreme act of holiness. In Judaism it is a *mitzvah*, a religious obligation. Judaism imbues the act of "accompaniment" with such importance that the rabbis elevated it among those very few religious obligations for which a person not only enjoys benefits in this world, but also receives their principal reward in the world-to-come.

One of my last visits in the late fall was to a nursing home facility where I was to play for a Mrs. Z. When I arrived late morning, I was told by the nurse that Mrs. Z. would likely not be in her room but sitting in a common room with the other residents. And when I arrived there she was, sitting at a table with three other residents. Many others were scattered about the room. Sadly, there was no television, no entertainment – no stimulation of any kind. Many residents simply were staring into space, some had their heads down on their chests, and others looking like their minds were in the twilight zone. I approached Mrs. Z and introduced myself. She was not conversant, but simply sat there but no verbal communication. The nurse asked whether she would like Mrs. Z. to be wheeled back to her room. I thought it would be just as easy to have her seated at her table, and for me to play for her in the common room. The nurse acquiesced and so I began to softly sing my first song: "You are my sunshine, you are my sunshine, you make me happy when skies are blue ... "

There was no visible response to my singing by Mrs. Z. which was of course disappointing, but I decided to persist with the experience of knowing that sometimes it takes a few more minutes or the just the "right" song to get a response.

Perhaps Mrs. Z was hearing impaired and I needed to sing a song using a louder voice. Or maybe I needed to figure out the song that would pique her interest and evoke a response. As it was approaching Thanksgiving, I thought that perhaps an American standard would be a good choice, and so I began in a much louder voice to sing "America the Beautiful."

> O beautiful for spacious skies for amber waves of
>   grain
> For purple mountains majesty above the fruited
>   plain....

Still no response from Mrs. Z. but when I glanced around the room, I noticed a couple of the residents who began to move their arms and sing along with me. I smiled and began to sing even with more volume the next verse:

> O beautiful for vision clear that sees beyond the
>   years
> Thy nighttime sky our hopes that fly undimmed by
>   human tears
> America America God shed his grace on thee
> 'Til selfish gain no longer stain the banner of the free.

Still no response from Mrs. Z. but some of those residents whose heads were bowed down to their chests awakened and began singing too. I decided to stand up this time so that everyone in the room could see me and with guitar pick in hand played and sang the familiar verse 1 as if I were singing for a venue at Madison Square Garden.

America, America God shed his grace on thee
And crown thy good with brotherhood from sea to
    shining sea.

By now I had most of those in the room singing and sway-ing to the music. Still extraordinarily little response from Mrs. Z. I decided to sing one more song – "That's Amore"

When the moon hits your eye like a big pizza pie that's
    amore
When the world seems to shine like you've had too much
    wine that's amore
Bells will ring ting-a-ling-a-ling ting-a-ling-a-ling and
    you'll sing vita bella
Hearts will play tippy-tippy-tay tippy-tippy-tay like a
    gay tarantella.

I felt like I now was leading the entire choir of the nursing home as this song seemed to grab most everyone – that is, except my patient Mrs. Z. I still felt that overall, this was a successful first visit to Mrs. Z. Perhaps she was hearing the music, but just not ready to react. Fortunately, there will be more times to visit her, and hopefully I will have better news to report moving forward. One thing is for certain. For me, seeing the awakening of the residents was a transcendental experience of the mind and spirit. Rabbi Nachman of Breslov who loved song said that "the most direct means of attaching ourselves to the spiritual is through music." I witnessed today firsthand Plato's thoughts regarding music: "music gives a soul to the universe, wings to the mind and life to everything."

Music has healing power. It has the ability to take people out of themselves for a few hours. (Elton John)

CHAPTER 6
Virtual Music

As the year 2020 commenced I continued to do my music visits at assisted living facilities, nursing homes and private homes. My relationships with many of my patients continued to blossom and I was very much enjoying my opportunities to offer them my music. Life for everyone around the world was about to change as the corona virus began to spread across the globe. It was not long before countries around the globe and the United States closed everything down with a stay at home order. Schools and places of worship closed, restaurants, retail stores, sporting events, theatre were all curtailed. Only essential workers were allowed to proceed with their jobs. I no longer was able to make personal visits to my people. I could only imagine their loneliness since not even family members were allowed to visit their loved ones. And so, each day many had to shelter in their rooms and wait for that call from a family member or the person who would come and bring them their meal or give them their medication.

A few weeks into the pandemic one of the hospice nurses texted me to suggest that perhaps I could do a virtual music visit with my patients. With the help of the hospice Executive Director and the coordination of the Program Director of a local Assisted Living facility I have been able to play and sing my music virtually, via FaceTime and Zoom. Families are now invited to join the sessions and to participate with their loved ones. This has been a win-win-win. The isolated patients enjoy and benefit from the engagement; the families get to see their beloved and join them in uplifting activity. I get to meet the family members, sometimes learn a bit of family history, and always share their joy in seeing their loved ones and reducing everyone's stress.

I recall a memorable virtual visit which took place on a Friday, the eve of the Jewish Sabbath. I played and sang for Mrs. B. a woman in her 90's. Her daughters, a granddaughter, and a great granddaughter joined the call. Great grandma smiled broadly, and her eyes lit up as she realized how many family members were on the screen. Tears flowed down my cheeks when, in keeping with their Sabbath family tradition, all of the family members joining in singing "Woman of Valor" – Eishes Chayil" (Proverbs 31) to great grandma. It was a transcendent experience.

As I write this chapter things are beginning to slowly open up in cities across the country, but only essential workers are still allowed to leave their homes to do their work. I am hopeful one day to going back to bring my guitar and song to the rooms and homes of my patients. There is nothing quite like being there physically, and occasionally getting to hold a patient's hand or offer them a glass of water. But for now, I am so very thankful that there is technology which allows me to extend my hand (virtually that is) and offer my music to my patients and their families.

Afterword

*I*t has been more than four years since I began my visiting patients in my role as Chords of Comfort. I am still amazed in having experienced firsthand how music and the mind intersect and how music can have healing power. All of my patients are in hospice and many of them have passed on since I first started playing music for them. I have fond memories of them and am hopeful that they are resting in peace. When a person is diagnosed with a disease that is likely to result in death, they are often referred to as being terminal. In such cases families may wish to choose care for their loved one that will give comfort and relief from the suffering, rather than attempting at eradicating disease. Hospice care is care of the whole person – body, emotions and spiritual life. It also includes caring for the ill person's family. I am one of several complementary providers that make up the hospice team for whom I work. Other team members include the patient and his or her loved ones, doctors, nurses, social workers, clergy, home health aides and volunteer visitors. Working together each strives to value the needs and wishes of the patient and family to empower them to make choices and implement solutions that are right for them.

Although most of us do not hesitate to visit close friends and family when they become ill, we are not always comfortable doing it. We are even less comfortable at the prospect of visiting casual friends or strangers. Almost all my patients were strangers to me when I met them for the first time. But as the Bible reminds us more than thirty-six times that we must reach out and help the stranger. It is a *mitzvah* (religious obligation) to visit the sick, and I have viewed my work as Chords of Comfort as mitzvah work. When I enter the room of one of my patients, I bring my presence and my capacity for love and compassion. For those who I have been fortunate enough to visit on numerous occasions, my singing and playing has offered the possibility of a healing relationship. I have learned that an attitude of hopefulness is possible even in dark times. The very presence of all of those who visit the sick (many synagogues have Visiting the Sick groups) shows that they are not alone and that we come as representatives of a caring community.

A piece in one of the major newspapers detailed the last day of the life of President George H. W. Bush. It described how in the last week of the President's life he had stopped eating and was mostly sleeping. Close friends visited him in his last days. One held his hand and rubbed his feet. The former President died in his home, surrounded by several close friends, family members, doctors and a minister. As the end of his life neared on a Friday, his son the former President George W. Bush was at his home in Dallas and was put on speaker phone to say his goodbye. He told his father that he was a "wonderful dad" and that he loved him. "I love you too" Mr. Bush told his son. And those were his final words. It was a graceful gentle death.

There is a rabbi who directs a Jewish-End-of-Life Care/ Hospice Volunteer program. As part of his training program, the rabbi asks the volunteers to reflect on a moment when they needed someone to be present for them. One man related the story of his bicycle accident when a stranger sat silently with him on the curb until the ambulance arrived. Another volunteer described how her grandfather sat knitting in the corner of the hospital's delivery room throughout her three-day-long labor. What both stories have in common is the power of someone simply being present for another person.

The word "companion" is derived from the Latin "com" ("with") and "panis" (bread). It literally means someone with whom you share bread. The Hebrew word for this concept is "levaya" (accompaniment). This concept is so central to how we think about death and dying in Judaism that we use the same Hebrew word (levaya) for "funeral." In Judaism we do not bury our death. We accompany them. And even before burial the custom is that once members of the Holy Burial Society have prepared the deceased for burial, they then remain present and "accompany" the deceased through the night by sitting with the body and reading from the Book of Psalms. Spiritual care is all about accompanying another person while being fully present. I am fortunate in that my accompaniment includes my song and my guitar which I have witnessed firsthand in its ability to help raise the spirits of my patients and offer them a modicum of comfort and healing. Even when someone's life is waning, healing of spirit is possible until their very last breath. Being there often raises my own spirits.

It has been a privilege and an honor to be one of my hospice's complementary providers, serving in my role as Chords of Comfort. I am looking forward to meeting more people and experiencing more adventures as I continue my work and sing my songs.

Many years ago, when my wife and I were dating, she crocheted for me a *yarmulke* in Hebrew with a verse from the Book of Psalms (104:33) which she thought would recognize my talents –

Ashira laShem B'chayai – I will sing to the Lord all the days of my life. I hope to do just that.

A Final Story:
The Spiritual Side
of Palliative Care:
"Give Me Your Hand"

The following Talmudic tales describe what occurs when a rabbi visits another rabbi who is ill.

The First Tale

Rabbi Hiyya fell ill and the great healer, Rabbi Yochanan went in to visit him. Yochanan went in to visit him and said: "Are your sufferings welcome to you?"

He replied: "Neither they nor their reward."

Then Yochanan said: "Give me your hand."

He gave him his hand and he raised him.

Second Tale

Once Rabbi Yochanan, the healer, fell ill and Rabbi Hanina went to visit him. He said to him: "Are your sufferings welcome to you?"

He replied: "Neither they nor their reward."
He said to him: "Give me your hand."
He gave him his hand and he raised him.
Why could not Rabbi Yochanan raise himself?
The prisoner cannot free himself from jail.

Third Tale
Another man, Rabbi Eleazar, fell ill and Rabbi Yochanan went in to visit him. Yochanan noticed that he was lying in a dark room, and he bared his arm and light radiated from it.

Thereupon, he noticed that Rabbi Eleazar was weeping, and he said to him: "Why do you weep? Is it because you did not study Torah? Surely, we learned: The one who sacrifices much and the one who sacrifices little have the same merit, provided that the heart is directed to heaven.

Is it perhaps lack of sustenance? Not everyone has the privilege to enjoy two tables.

Is it perhaps because of the lack of children? This is the bone of my tenth son!"

Rabbi Eleazar replied to him: "I am weeping on account of this beauty that is going to rot in the earth."

Yochanan said to him: "On that account you surely have a reason to weep." And they both wept.

In the meanwhile, he said to him: "Are your sufferings welcome to you?

Eleazar replied: "Neither they nor their reward."

Yochanan said to him: "Give me your hand," and he gave him his hand and raised him.

(Talmud, Berachot 5)

Jewish tradition teaches that it is important to allow others to help us when we are sick. According to the three tales Rabbi Yochanan visited Rabbi Hanina during the latter's illness.

When Rabbi Hanina complained about his suffering, Rabbi Yochanan suggested that he speak the same encouraging words to himself that he had spoken with such good effect to Rabbi Yochanan when he was ill. Rabbi Hanina replied: "When I was free of sufferings, I could help others. But now that I am myself a sufferer, I must ask others to help me."

The meaning of the story is critical to understand the importance of visiting the sick. We should know both how to give and how to take, and that in taking, often we are also giving. By giving one's hand, a person can raise one's spirits and bring both physical and psychological healing. A sick person cannot heal himself but needs the help of others. In the Talmudic tales Rabbi Yochanan's healing addressed both his friend's suffering and pain, making his actions a fine example of the palliative care approach.

In my role of Chords of Comfort, I have had the opportunity to see firsthand the power of music in healing the body, mind and spirit. In visiting the sick there is a benefit that flows not only to the person who is ill but to you, the visitor. It is as if you were the one who asked the patient, "Give me your hand," and rose up stronger and straighter because of the touch. There is a Jewish teaching that each soul is so precious that God has assigned a team of angels to watch over each human being. Some of them are even musical angels, known for their beautiful singing voices. These angels are always looking for more volunteers. Seize the opportunity. If not now, when?